How Full is Full?

Comparing Bodies of Water

Vic Parker

www.raintreepublishers.co.uk
Visit our website to find out more information about Raintree books.

To order:
☏ Phone 0845 6044371
🗎 Fax +44 (0) 1865 312263
🖳 Email myorders@raintreepublishers.co.uk

Customers from outside the UK please telephone +44 1865 312262

Raintree is an imprint of Capstone Global Library Limited, a company incorporated in England and Wales having its registered office at 7 Pilgrim Street, London, EC4V 6LB – Registered company number: 6695582

Edited by Nancy Dickmann, Rebecca Rissman, and Sian Smith
Designed by Victoria Allen
Picture research by Hannah Taylor
Original illustrations © Capstone Global Library 2011
Original illustrations by Victoria Allen
Production by Victoria Fitzgerald
Originated by Dot Gradations Ltd
Printed and bound in China by South China Printing Company Ltd

ISBN 978 0 431 00606 2 (hardback)
14 13 12 11 10
10 9 8 7 6 5 4 3 2 1

ISBN 978 1 406 21955 5 (paperback)
15 14 13 12 11
10 9 8 7 6 5 4 3 2 1

British Library Cataloguing in Publication Data
Parker, Victoria.
 How full is full? : comparing bodies of water. -- (Measuring and comparing)
 1. Volume (Cubic content)--Measurement--Juvenile literature.
 I. Title II. Series
 530.8-dc22

Acknowledgements
The author and publisher are grateful to the following for permission to reproduce copyright material: © Capstone Publishers pp.4, 5, 8, 26, 27 (Karon Dubke); Corbis pp.7 (Bo Zaunders), 12 (David Shopper), 22 (Tom Van Sant); Getty Images p.25 (Chris Sattlberger); istockphoto pp.6 (© Timothy Goodwin), 14 (© Fabien Courtitarat), 20 (© Arpad Benedek); Photolibrary pp.10 (Stephen Beaudet), 16 (Tips Italia/ Bildagentur RM), 18 (Britain on View); shutterstock pp.24 (© Sally Scott).

Photographs used to create silhouettes: istockphoto, bath (© Brandi Powell); shutterstock, bucket (© Matthew Cole), child (© Robert Adrian Hillman), fish (© stock09), swimmers (© gaga), reeds (© Kaetana), boats (© sabri denic kizil).

Cover photograph of a courtyard with a fountain reproduced with permission of Photolibrary (Garden Picture Library/ Andrea Jones).

Every effort has been made to contact copyright holders of material reproduced in this book. Any omissions will be rectified in subsequent printings if notice is given to the publisher.

Contents

Words appearing in the text in bold, like this,
are explained in the glossary.

Measuring capacity

A liquid is something runny, such as water or milk. Liquids can fill up containers. The total space for liquid inside a container is called its **capacity**.

Containers come in many different shapes and sizes.

Liquids are usually measured in litres (l).
Small amounts can be measured in millilitres (ml).
There are 1,000 millilitres in a litre.

To measure small amounts, we can use measuring cups or jugs.

What is a body of water?

A body of water is any amount of water in one place. A body of water can be big, such as an ocean or a sea. A body of water can be small, such as a pond or a puddle.

A puddle is a small, shallow body of water.

We use bodies of water in many ways. You can swim in a swimming pool or a lake. Boats sail on rivers, lakes, and oceans. They carry people and **goods** from place to place.

A huge amount of our planet is covered with water, so boats can be a good way to travel.

A glass of water

Have you ever measured how much water a glass can hold? Compared to a spoon, it can hold a lot. But what can hold more water than a glass?

Some glasses hold about 400 millilitres of water.

A bucket can hold more than a glass of water. Most buckets hold about 12 litres. It would take around 30 glasses of water to hold as much water as a full bucket.

30 glasses of water

1 bucket of water

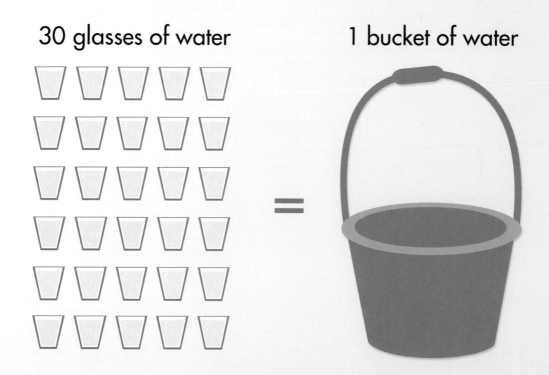

=

What can hold more water than a bucket? ➡

A bath

A bath can hold more than a bucket. Baths come in lots of different shapes and sizes. A bath with a person in it cannot hold as much water as when no one is in it.

Taking a bath can be a fun way to keep clean!

A regular-sized bath can hold about 200 litres of water. If you tried to fill up a bath by using buckets of water, you would need about 16 full buckets.

16 buckets of water

1 bath of water

=

What can hold more water than a bath? ➡️

A fish pond

A pond in a garden can hold more than a bath. Many people like having a small pond in their garden. You can also find ponds in parks.

A pond can be a home for fish.

Fish ponds can be different shapes and sizes. A small pond might hold about 6,000 litres of water. This is as much water as 30 baths.

30 baths of water

the water in 1 fish pond

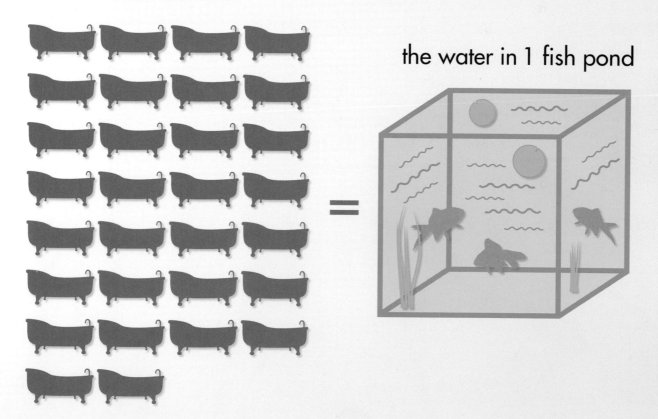

=

What can hold more water than a fish pond? ➡

A swimming pool

A swimming pool can hold more than a fish pond. An Olympic-sized swimming pool can hold a huge amount of water – about two million, five hundred thousand litres!

Olympic-sized pools are often used for swimming races.

If you wanted to fill up an Olympic swimming pool by using fish ponds full of water, you would need about 416 full fish ponds.

the water in 1 Olympic swimming pool

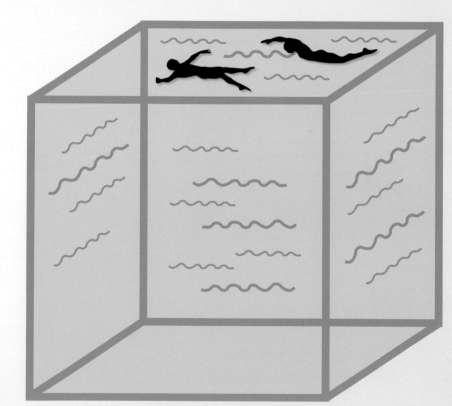

the water in 1 fish pond

What can hold more water than a swimming pool? ➡

A canal lock

A canal lock can hold more than a swimming pool. Canals look like rivers, but they are built by people. A lock is a part of a canal that can be closed off by gates.

A lock can take boats down to a lower canal level, or raise them up to a higher canal level.

A canal lock must be big enough to hold a boat. Some of the biggest locks hold as much water as 40 full Olympic-sized swimming pools.

the water in 1 large canal lock

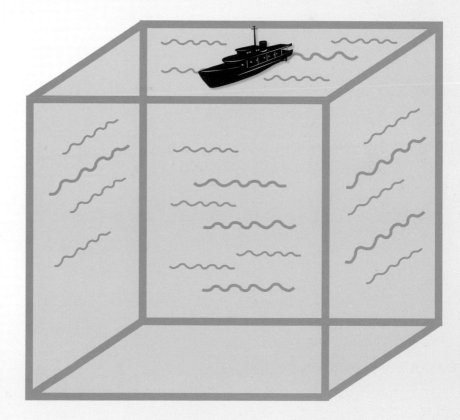

the water in 1 Olympic swimming pool

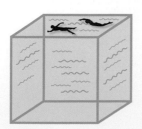

What can hold more water than a canal lock? ➡️

A reservoir

A **reservoir** can hold more than a **canal lock**.
A reservoir is a natural or man-made pool.
Most reservoirs are made when a **dam** is
built to block a river.

Reservoirs are built to hold
water that can later be
used in people's homes.

dam

Clywedog
reservoir

Clywedog (pronounced 'Cluw-ed-og') reservoir is a fairly small reservoir in Wales. Even so, you would need the water from about 500 large canal locks to fill the Clywedog reservoir.

the water in Clywedog reservoir

the water in 1 large canal lock

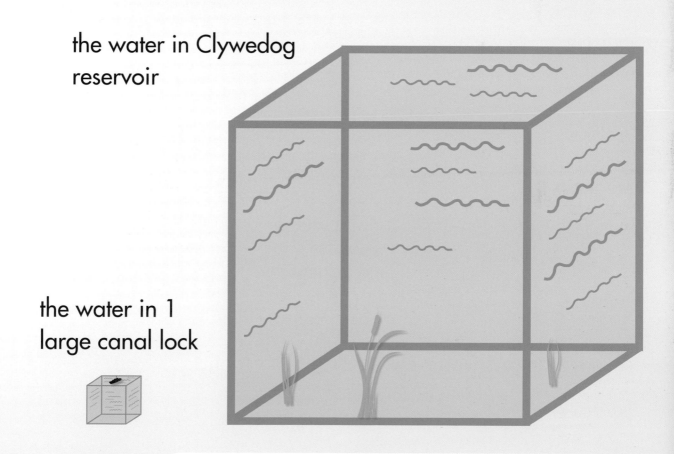

What can hold more water than a reservoir? ➡

A lake

A lake can hold more than a **reservoir**. A lake is a large body of water that is surrounded by land on all sides. Lake Superior is one of the world's largest lakes.

Lake Superior lies between Canada and the United States.

Lake Superior is so enormous that in some places, you cannot see from one side of it to the other. It would take 242,000 Clywedog reservoirs to fill Lake Superior.

the water in Lake Superior

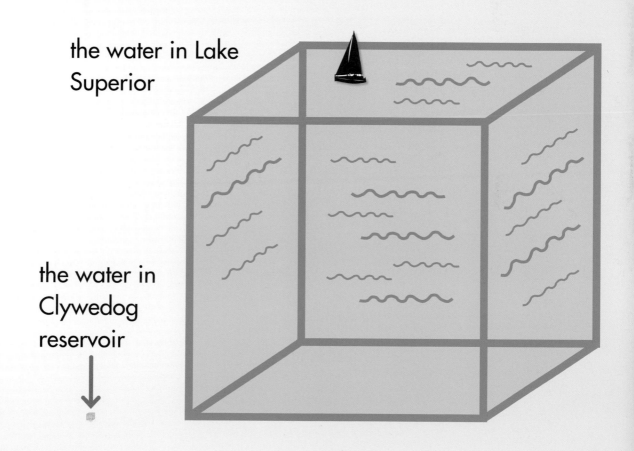

the water in Clywedog reservoir

What can hold more water than a lake?

A sea

A sea can hold more than a lake. A sea is a body of moving water connected to a bigger ocean. The Mediterranean is a sea that feeds into the Atlantic Ocean.

The water in the Mediterranean Sea is salty, like the water in the ocean.

ATLANTIC OCEAN

Europe

Asia

MEDITERRANEAN SEA

Africa

The Mediterranean Sea lies between southern Europe, western Asia, and northern Africa. It would take more than 347 Lake Superiors to fill the Mediterranean Sea.

the water in the Mediterranean Sea

the water in Lake Superior

What can hold more water than a sea? ➡

An ocean

An ocean is bigger than a sea. The largest ocean on Earth is the Pacific Ocean. It contains more than half of all the water on Earth.

The Pacific Ocean covers about one-third of the Earth's surface.

It would take more than 160 Mediterranean Seas to fill the Pacific Ocean. That's more than three trillion, four hundred billion (3,400,000,000,000) baths!

The Pacific Ocean is so big that it can take several weeks to sail across it.

Measuring activity

Things you will need: water, a 1 litre measuring jug, and containers of different shapes and sizes (see-through ones are best). For example: a cup, a shallow dish, a deep bowl, and a tall thin vase.

(1) Fill the measuring jug to the 250 millilitres mark.

(2) Pour your 250 millilitres of water into one of the containers.

③ Fill the jug with another 250 millilitres of water and pour it into another one of the containers.

④ Do the same until all of the containers have 250 millilitres of water in them.

Find out: Does it look as though there is the same amount of water in each container?

Full quiz and facts

Measuring liquid
Small amounts are measured in millilitres (ml).
Larger amounts are measured in litres (l).

Remember
1,000 millilitres (ml) = 1 litre (l)

Quiz

1. What unit would you use to measure the amount of water in a paddling pool?
   a) millilitres   b) litres

2. What unit would you use to measure the amount of water in one raindrop?
   a) millilitres   b) litres

Answers: 1 = b   2 = a

Full facts

- Loch Ness is a famous lake in Scotland. There is a greater amount of water in Loch Ness than in all the lakes in England and Wales put together.

- The Caspian Sea is the world's largest lake.

- There are five oceans on Earth. The largest ocean is the Pacific Ocean.

- Very large amounts of water are measured in **cubic** kilometres. Imagine a huge cube made of water. If all the sides of the cube were one kilometre long, that would be one cubic kilometre of water.

- Lake Nasser is a huge **reservoir** which was created when the Aswan **Dam** was built across the River Nile. It holds 132 cubic kilometres of water.

- There are a whopping three hundred and fifty-four million and seven hundred thousand cubic kilometres of water in the Atlantic Ocean.

Glossary

canal man-made body of water, similar to a river

capacity the maximum amount that something will hold. A container's capacity is the biggest amount that the container can hold.

cubic shaped like a cube. Most dice are shaped like cubes. Every side on a cube is the same length.

dam strong wall that is built across a river or stream to trap water

goods things that people buy or sell, such as food or clothes

lock part of a canal that can be closed off by gates. Locks are used to move ships up or down to different levels of the canal.

reservoir large lake used to hold water that can later be used in people's homes and businesses. Natural lakes are sometimes made into reservoirs or reservoirs are built by people.

Find out more

Books

I Wonder Why the Sea is Salty: and Other Questions About the Oceans, Anita Ganeri (Kingfisher Books, 2003)

Oceans (My World of Geography), Vic Parker (Raintree Publishers, 2005)

Water (Investigate), Charlotte Guillain (Raintree Publishers, 2009)

Websites

www.bbc.co.uk/skillswise/e3/numbers/
measuresshapespace/capacity
Learn about capacity through the factsheet, quiz, and measuring game on this website.

www.metoffice.gov.uk/education/kids/weather_
experiments_puddle.html
Try out the puddle experiment on this website.

Index